EVERY EXCUSE IN THE BOOK

EVERY EXCUSE IN THE BOOK

Marc Juris and Cindy Kuris

ISBN: 1-55547-243-5

Manufactured in the United States of America

TABLE OF CONTENTS

Introduction vii
Good reasons why you were late to work 9
A look back: The history of creative excuse-making 14
Quiz—What's your HFQ? (Honesty factor quotient) 17
Believable scenarios which caused you to miss
a day of work 20
Mix and match: Excuses for any occasion 25
Foolproof explanations for denting the car 27
Passing the buck & other popular excuse strategies 30
Convenient reasons for why you didn't pay a bill 33
A must-have list of supplies for effective
excuse-making 35
Extraordinary tales for leaving anyplace immediately . . . 37
The other half of today's most popular fibs 41
Gut wrenching reasons for why the check bounced 43
Excuses in the professional world 46
All in a day's work—A guide to job titles and what
they really mean 48
Simple reasons for not having that paper or report 49
Excuses and your state of mind 52
Excuses and the state you're in 53
Unfortunate circumstances which caused you to
gain weight 55
Advice from the experts 56
The white lie vs. the black lie 63
Prescription vacations 64
Seemingly plausible reasons for ending your
relationship 66
Absolutely legal reasons for exceeding the speed
limit 70
Brilliant explanations for killing the dog or cat 73
How to talk yourself out from between a rock and a
hard place 76
Excellent reasons for getting off the phone 78

Meeting your match: How to tell if someone is handing you a line 81

Easy-to-use explanations for not returning a call 84

Making the best of a bad situation—A guide to solving some everyday problems 86

Handy stories for breaking a date 88

Living, loving, lying: The importance of creating an intriguing, but false, past, present, and future 91

Very good reasons why you got home late or never got home at all 93

Creative excuse-making: Do's and Don'ts 98

Solid reasons why you are unemployed 100

Why I can't visit you, Mom 102

More advice from the experts 103

More good reasons why you were late 107

More excuses to get the whole day off 111

More random excuses 114

More of why the car is dented 115

Further reasons for that bill not being paid 117

More reasons you don't have the report/paper 119

More reasons why you suddenly gained weight 121

More expert tips 123

More reasons why the relationship has to end 126

More stories for breaking a date 127

INTRODUCTION

Creative excuse-making, effective fact manipulation, speaking with a forked tongue, hogwashing, or whatever you want to call it, downright lying is the single most maligned and underdeveloped aspect of our personality.

Used properly, an excuse allows you the freedom to increase your leisure time, command a higher salary, dump ugly dates, deal with shifty auto-mechanics, or even, with fluency in a foreign language, take control of a small country. The consummate excuse-maker knows how to maximize personal gain without ever being considered cruel, cheap, or irresponsible.

At this stage, somewhere in your subconscious, you may be resisting this line of reasoning. After all, an excuse is a lie and lying is wrong. Please, don't be so naive.

From the moment a child is born, parents and teachers unite to drum into a child's small head what a terrible thing it is to tell a lie. His nose will grow, his tongue will freeze, everyone will reject him and worse, he'll be forced to pursue a career in local politics.

Not only is this unfair to the child (who'll never learn how to prepare an effective resume), but it's also hypocritical— No one tells more lies than a mother.

Learning the art of creative-excuse-making is very simple and, with a little practice, should come as natural as a seizure. That's why we've brought you this book. Within these pages are excuses for absolutely, positively every cotton-picking occasion when a little story beats the hell out of telling the truth.

GOOD REASONS WHY YOU WERE
LATE TO WORK

I went out to my car this morning only to find that it:
a) was stolen
b) was towed
c) was fire-bombed
d) had a dead battery
e) was full of water
f) was upside down
g) had no steering wheel
h) had no wheels at all
i) was turned into a convertible by a low flying plane
j) had a shopping bag lady sleeping in it and will have to be
   professionally fumigated

My mother called at 6:00 A.M. to tell me that she decided to
go back to my father. I was so groggy that I gave her my
blessing, not realizing my father died six years ago. Naturally, I'm running out the door to find poor old mom. Do you
know where the nearest Arthur Murray Tango Room is?

It's the strangest thing, but my feet swelled up and now I
can't get my shoes on. I'm sure I'll be in within a couple of
hours.

A McDonald's trainee accidentally put secret sauce on my
Egg McMuffin. Now, I'm not only violently ill, but also
developing a strange resemblance to Mayor McCheese.

I had to take my spouse/roommate to the emergency room last night after he/she:
a) fell out of the window
b) swallowed a spoon
c) accidentally ate a tampax
d) got hit by a car
e) got hit by me
f) got hit by the mob
g) confessed his or her lust for Ed McMahon

My true love actually had the nerve to send me a partridge in a pear tree. The damn bird has ruined my living room rug and I'm waiting for the trucking company to get the thing out of here.

My niece spent the night and woke up convinced she was the devil. Don't ask, all I know is that I'm waiting for her mother to come get her out of here. By the way, do you know how to get green vomit out of dacron?

(Speak into the phone with a brush handle in your mouth.) Listen, I know this sounds crazy but I've gotten my lip frozen to the ice tray—be in soon, I hope.

Last night, during a violent coughing fit, my left eye fell out. Thank God for the modern wonders of medicine, all is well, except for this uncontrollable urge to buy Sammy Davis records.

I'll be in a little late this morning. The piano fell on my dog.

Hi, I'm calling from a pay phone and, well, I'll be a little late. You see, I'm waiting for the phone company to send someone to pry my finger from the coin slot.

Believe it or not, there is a big, drunk, angry black man outside my door demanding to see his mother. I'm not sure, but I think he has a knife. Or is it a bottle of Ripple?

You won't believe this. My parakeet exploded.

Although they assured me delivery before 9 A.M., I'm still waiting for my new:
a) Sofa
b) Inflatable Wife
c) Refrigerator
d) Foster Child
e) Dolly Parton Jell-O Mold
f) Home Heart Transplant Set
g) 100% Virgin Orlon Sweater Set
h) Marble Bust of Ed Sullivan
i) Dave Del Dotto Cash Flow System
j) Fudgie the Whale Anniversary Cake

When I woke up this morning I noticed that during the night I swallowed all of my caps. That's the last time I go to a dentist who advertises on Elvira's Fright Night Theater.

My mother insists that she saw an alien coming out of a space ship when she was throwing out the garbage. Now I have to take her to see Steven Spielberg's agent. I don't know, everyone thinks they've got the next E.T.!

It just hit me that John Lennon is dead. Look, I really can't deal with it. I just needed an hour or two to get my head together.

On the way to the office I spotted a $5 bill on the street. I bent down to pick it up and my pants split wide open. I swear there was a crew from the David Letterman Show who definitely got the whole thing on tape.

A LOOK BACK: THE HISTORY
OF EXCUSE-MAKING

Hundreds of billions of years ago, before there were countries, cities, corporations or a department of motor vehicles, a universe was created. As with any major universe, the first few days were a bit slow: Man seemed content gathering roots and berries, breaking the monotony with an occasional hand wash at the river's edge.

"Things take time," our creator reasoned.

After a few more days, the creator looked back down only to find his people not making the progress he had imagined. "A bunch of lazy slobs!" he muttered, "and to think I had projected solid room deodorizers by the mid 1600's."

Confused and rejected, the creator put away the rough drafts for the first Twinkie, defeated in his attempts to figure out how to get the creme in the cake without leaving a trace, when it hit him. Communication! That's what he needed to build a great world. A world where two great comediennes, Lavernius and Shirlius, would one day rise to fame and entertain millions.

Faced with this problem of communication, the creator carefully considered several options; bone-cracking, hair-positioning, and foot-stomping (immediately ruled out and reserved for mathematical questions posed to a horse). The creator needed something more flexible, yet cost-efficient. And so he decided upon tone-exchanging.

Equipping each human with a voice box and a voice modulating contouring device (later changed to "tongue" when delicatessen owners complained they couldn't fit it on their take-out menu boards), each person was now prepared to communicate his feelings. But this constant groaning, though suitable for government employees, soon proved to have significant limitations. So the creator developed the word "abcdefghijklmnopqrstuvwxyz."

However, because he could develop only 100 different inflections, and therefore only 100 meanings, the creator decided to break the word down, calling its components "letters," the merging of two or more letters "words," and the merging of ten or more letters "medical terms."

Armed with the necessary variables to create literally thousands of words, as well as developing a new concept for a breakfast cereal, the creator had given birth to the vocabulary.

The trouble was that by the time all this came to pass, the sixth day had slipped by. It was now Sunday, the universal day of rest (except for those who work in major department stores) and the creator was forced to leave the responsibility of enforcing the rules of languages to human beings.

Left with the task of policing the vocabulary, men divided into two types, honest moral man and truth distorting man (commonly referred to as advertising executives). From this point in history to present there has been a battle between the two, with honest moral man typically inventing stories about the evils of lying and truth distorting man generally living a happier, more fulfilling life.

WHAT'S YOUR HFQ—
(HONESTY FACTOR QUOTIENT?)

So you think you always tell the truth? This brief quiz will tell you how honest you really are:

Have you ever told a dear friend that her new hairdo looks great even though it looks as if her head fell in a Cuisinart?
a) Yes   b) No

Have you ever told a child any of the following:
a) The Boogie Man will come get him if he doesn't go to bed.
b) You'll turn the car around and return home if he doesn't stop chewing on his sister's hair.
c) That you'll break his neck.
d) That he'll go blind if he doesn't keep his hands out of a certain area.
e) That his baby brother or sister came from a Sear's catalogue.

Have you ever returned a clothing item to a department store, claiming it was defective, even though it was you who accidentally put it in the dishwasher?
a) Yes   b) No

Have you ever knowingly written a check without sufficient funds to cover it?
a) Yes   b) No

As a child did you ever break an item in your parent's home and then do one of the following:
a) Throw it out, thinking your mother would forget she ever owned such a hideous thing.
b) Put it back together, hoping mom would think she broke it while dusting.

Have you ever told a friend that she hasn't gained an ounce, even though you originally thought she swallowed a Winnebago?
a) Yes   b) No

Have you ever made a phone call and, upon finding the party not home, called the operator and told her you reached a wrong number?
a) Yes   b) No

Have you ever had a premeditated arrangement with your mother to call her person-to-person from your dead uncle so she could call you back at the direct dial rate?
a) Yes   b) No

Have your ever called in sick, even though you were in Wildwood, New Jersey, eating a potato knish on the boardwalk?
a) Yes   b) No

Score 1 for each "Yes" answer.

Your Score: 1-2   HFQ#1
                       3-5   HFQ#2
                       5-7   HFQ#3
                       8-9   HFQ#4

EVALUATING YOUR SCORE

HFQ 1 As honest as you believed yourself to be, you do have the tendency to blurt out a little excuse now and then. You probably donate money to the 700 Club through your local television station, and are best suited to be a librarian or a mud analyst for a major chemical company.

HFQ 2 You are inventive and possess a crude mastery of the language. You can get yourself out of a good number of situations, but not all. You've probably stolen a magazine out of a doctor's office on occasion and are best suited to be a building superintendent or a salesman in the garment industry.

HFQ 3 You have a strong command in the art of excuse-making and really know how to get what you want out of life. You are best suited to be an entrepreneur, a leader of a fanatical religious cult or a real estate broker.

HFQ 4 You are truly a remarkable person. Cunning, clever, and devious, you can get anything out of anyone at any time. You are best suited to be a theatrical agent, a public relations whiz kid, or a scheduler of furniture deliveries for a major department store.

BELIEVABLE SCENARIOS
WHICH CAUSED YOU TO MISS A DAY OF WORK

Remember when I went to that hypnotist to stop smoking? Well, he must have made a mistake because I was walking out the door feeling great, when suddenly, the next thing I knew I was in the hospital. The doctors told me it took three men to remove me from the frozen food section of a supermarket where I was telling people I was Mama Celeste and forcing them to buy my Pizzas For One.

Early this morning I was arrested for ripping all the tags off my living room sofa. I'm at the police station now and they only allowed me one call, so can you do me a favor? Call a bail bondsman.

My fat Aunt Louise was over for dinner last night and somehow got wedged in between the toilet bowl and the bathtub. I spent the whole night prying her loose and threw my back out.

Last night I was kidnapped by a gay cab driver. Believe it or not, he actually took me to his mother's house and forced me to pose as his fiancée. Then, he made me stay the night helping him pick out wall paper patterns for the baby's room. Take it from me, never take a gypsy cab.

Last night, I woke up in the middle of the night and began to:
a) throw up

b) sweat profusely
c) scream in pain
d) scream in French

During my shower this morning, I accidentally used my wife's (roommate's) depilatory cream. What did I know? It looked like shampoo. Anyway, now I'm completely bald and not going anywhere until my wig is ready.

I was using my seal-a-meal last night, and I'm not quite sure what happened, but I inadvertently sealed my hair into a bag of beef goulash. Oh, I've been meaning to ask you, how about a nice Hungarian dinner at my place tonight?

Gee, I don't know why, but I just plain thought it was Saturday.

21

While I was on the train I accidentally slammed my briefcase (pocketbook) into a dwarf. I apologized, but apparently it wasn't enough because he started biting my knee. My God, it was like having a Pit Bull strapped to my leg. Don't let those little guys fool you; they pack quite a punch.

I just discovered that my mother was a Nazi war criminal. It really shocked me, though now that I think about it, I kinda thought she was a little too strict about keeping my room clean. Anyway, I'm off to the shrink.

I accidentally flushed my wig/toupee down the toilet.

I know this is going to sound gross, but I have a hair growing out of my eye. Anyway, I've got to go to the doctor, and then

I'm going to run over to the *National Enquirer* and try and sell the story.

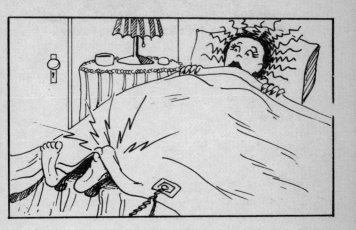

I was kept up the whole night by these bizarre electric shocks running through my body. I thought I was having a heart attack, until this morning, when I realized my big toe was stuck in the controls of my electric blanket.

I just found out my mother-in-law is a man. I wonder what size suit she wears?

A circus elephant got loose last night and stepped on my car.

I wasn't paying attention this morning and I accidentally shaved off my eyebrows. I look really strange and don't think

I'm going any where for a while. Do you think I could get a bit part in *Star Trek 4*?

I accidentally took a handful of Ex-Lax instead of my vitamins. Believe me, you don't want me around today.

MIX & MATCH: EXCUSES FOR ANY OCCASION

Not in the mood to go to work? Want out of a lousy date? Is the thought of going to your Aunt Henrietta's annual Polka party making you ill? Relax, this handy mix and match chart will get you out of absolutely anything. As a great Chinese wise man once said: "Pick one from column 'A' and one from column 'B'."

—HANDY MIX AND MATCH CHART—

Column "A"	Column "B"
Deranged woman screaming in center of freeway/street	Caused bus to overturn and throw you 6 blocks

Truckload of margarine exploding suddenly	Caused car to skid into a Taco Rico
Elvis Impersonator	Created mass hysteria
Young punk vandals roaming the street	Somehow set your toupee on fire
A staple gun sniper shooting #6 staples randomly in street	Hit you and forced you to seek a chiropracter for emergency treatment

FOOLPROOF EXPLANATIONS
FOR DENTING THE CAR

I stopped at (fill in name of local strip) to pick up a newspaper. Well, when I came out of the store, a bunch of hoods were break dancing on the car. I asked them to please stop, and LeVar, he's the leader, asked me if I wanted my face rearranged. Well, they **were** playing some good songs, so why stop the kids from having a good time?

I was on the highway minding my own business, when this woman dropped her bag of groceries from an overpass. Suddenly, a cantaloupe flew off the bridge and hit the car. It was such a shock. I didn't even know they were in season.

I was in the parking lot at the supermarket when a shopping cart mysteriously went berserk and started slamming itself right into the car. I'm not kidding, that cart was out to get me. By the way, do we have a Ouija board?

I'm never getting in that car again. It was driving like a dream, when all of a sudden, the steering wheel fell off in my hands. Thank God I wasn't going that fast and the Burger King Drive-Thru broke the impact.

I was sitting at a red light, perfectly motionless, when this deranged woman started hacking at the car with an ax. Don't think I was getting out to stop her. The really scary part was that she looked a lot like your mother. By the way, where was she today?

I was parked outside a Weight Watchers clinic and a fat man fell on the car. What was I gonna do, ask him for his registration?

I was going through a toll booth, and I guess I wasn't going fast enough because the gate came crashing down on the car. Either that, or someone figured out I threw Bolivian Centavos in the exact change basket.

You know that new Ted Turner satellite? Well, I think a piece of it fell off and hit the car. Forget about the dent, that can be fixed. It's the radio I'm worried about. Now it only picks up re-runs of Green Acres.

I went to the car wash and they accidentally hot waxed the tires. All of a sudden, the car flew off the conveyor belt and slid all the way into a busload of Korean grocers on their way to a produce convention.

That's not a dent, that's the design of the car.

PASSING THE BUCK & OTHER POPULAR
EXCUSE STRATEGIES

We all know that an excuse is an excuse is an excuse. But what many of us don't realize is the wide range of excuses one can choose from. For example, avoiding a date by saying you developed a boil on your lip is clearly different from shooting your ex-husband and claiming you were just "cleaning the gun." Situation, magnitude, and possible mental illness, are all factors in determining the type of excuse you'll use. Experts in the field of creative excuse-making (all of whom used to be cable television service representatives) have broken down excuses into the following categories:

THE FLASH—A panic-induced excuse, the Flash is a common response when a person's story is challenged and he has no time to get his story straight. It often begins "I, I, I, . . ." and then degenerates into something wildly stupid, very embarrassing and highly improbable. "I fell asleep in the car," was one man's flash when his wife asked him why he went off to the supermarket at 7:30 P.M. and didn't return until the following Thursday at noon. Fortunately, this man was lucky. His wife was stupid enough to believe him, though she did eventually leave him to become a hostess on "Wheel of Fortune."

THE TWIST—One of the most common forms of excuse-making, the Twist is simply a variation of the truth. A person who twists changes just one element of the story to give the impression of a completely different situation. "I'm late because I ran out of gas on the highway" just doesn't sound as good as its twisted version, "I'm late because my car exploded."

THE SLIP—Common in urban areas where people tend to talk very quickly, the Slip is the insertion of some very crucial point into the middle of a very long-winded sentence, hoping that the listener will not notice. "Oh! I had a marvelous day, picked up some of those delicious apples you love, met Aunt Henrietta for lunch, completely demolished your car, and, oh, I was wondering, do you want to see a show tonight?" This is just one example of how important information can be "slipped" to an unsuspecting patsy.

THE WHO, ME?—Another favorite, the Who, Me? is used in situations where a person was supposed to do something, but didn't. The idea is to pretend you honestly thought someone else was going to handle the situation. Also included in this category is the "You Never Told Me To Do That," and the "I Thought **You** Were Going To Do It," both of which seem to be very popular among employees of banks and Blue Cross/Blue Shield.

THE PASS THE BUCK—This type of excuse involves passing all blame and responsibility to an unsuspecting third party. At this time you must either: 1) convince this other person that you did in fact tell him to take care of the matter, or, 2) hope that he gets hit by a stray racquetball and is permanently convinced he's Uncle Joe from Petticoat Junction.

THE LOST IN SPACE—A favorite of psychotics and defense attorneys, the Lost In Space does not involve denial, but rather a shift in blame . . . to toasters, dogs, electric

31

currents seeping through walls or any other strange occurrence which cannot be proved. The goal here is not to get off the hook, but to guarantee yourself a few years rest at a quiet place in the country.

CONVENIENT REASONS
FOR WHY YOU DIDN'T PAY A BILL

Darling, all my bills are handled by my accountant. As soon as he returns from holiday in Peru I'll have him look into this sordid little matter. I simply must get off the phone now, my Bon-Bons are melting. Tata!

I accidentally spilled a carton of crazy glue all over my home and permanently bonded my fingers together. It's been murder trying to write, so I'm going in for surgery in a few weeks. As soon as I recuperate, I'll be happy to send you a check. Provided, of course, they can pry my legs off the breakfront.

Have a friend call and tell your creditor that you're in a coma. As soon as you come to, you'll send in your payment.

I invested all my money in C.D.'s at a local bank. Well, when I went to make a withdrawal, I was shocked to learn that at this bank a C.D. stands for chancy deposit. Now all my money's gone. And to think I didn't even take the damn blender.

Bill, what bill? Oh, so that's what the dog threw up the other day!

I got hit by a runaway bowling ball last week and now I can't remember who I am. I'd love to send you a check, but I don't even know my name. Besides, I certainly don't recall ever spending $3,000 on a collection of Eleanor Roosevelt commemorative plates.

A psychic advised me not to pay any bills for three months, or the person who receives the money will suffer a tragic death. I'm willing to take a chance—if you are.

Gee, silly me, I thought there was a mail strike.

A MUST HAVE LIST OF SUPPLIES FOR EFFECTIVE EXCUSE-MAKING

CAR— A car is perhaps the single most important device for effective excuse-making. It can break down, stall, stammer, sputter, and cause you to be hours late and unable to call. Owning a car opens a world of highways, auto mechanics, and poorly attended garages as the prime blamee for your misfortune. Only with a car can you sit comfortably with a friend, sipping a banana daiquiri, knowing that your wife will not rip your head off for shirking the responsibility of delivering the cold cuts to her Tupperware party.

MOTHER— Simply a must for excuse-making. No one can deny a child the right to run to his mother's aid when her luck is down. Illness, mental incompetence, and pathetic misfortune all work like a dream in any social or business situation when it happens to a lovable mom. So put your mother in a faulty respirator and enjoy a life of doing whatever you like.

DEAD PEOPLE— It's no secret that dead people are an invaluable tool to both novice and professional excuse-makers. Throughout this great nation schools echo with students confiding to their professors that the sudden death of grandpa or grandma has prevented them from completing that 70 page term paper on the use of adverbs in prehistoric Zimbabwee. When a person close to you dies, be sure not to tell a soul and save this tragic news for when it really counts. "Be inventive with your dead people and you can use them forever," said a noted authority on excuse-making and close personal friend of Stephen King. Remember, ghosts, ghouls, and demons can always come out to haunt you, and regardless of how crazy people think you are, they could never be mad for completely forgetting it was your day to car pool.

AMNESIA— An incredible, effortless, and easy tool, Amnesia is a down and dirty way to get out of absolutely anything. The beauty of amnesia is that you can always have a relapse and forget something new. No one can deny the amnesia patient every right to completely erase his responsibilities and any person relying on this person should be cautioned well in advance of any potential problems. That is, of course, if you can remember to tell them.

ILLNESS— This is a real building-block of excuse-making and requires very little set-up. Illness can strike anywhere, at any time, and anyway you like. From flu to bunions to rare skin diseases, a phony illness can provide for extended vacations, days in the park or brunch and an afternoon matinee. Don't overdo it though. With too many bizarre illnesses, people will be afraid to hang around you. And what's the point of a day off if you have no one to play with?

EXTRAORDINARY TALES FOR LEAVING
ANYPLACE IMMEDIATELY

Listen, I don't want to alarm you, but I'm having an out of body experience. Oh, it's nothing to worry about, it's just that every once in a while my soul leaves my body. By the way, I simply adore the towels in your bathroom. See what I mean?

What time is it? OH NO, YOU'RE KIDDING! Listen, I've got to go:
a) feed the cat
b) feed the dog
c) feed the cat to the dog

Oh no, I completely forgot to return the car I rented. I better get it back before they charge me for an extra day. By the way, can I borrow a couple of bucks for gas?

You probably won't relate to this, but I'm getting a strong message from God that I must go to church and pray immediately.

Look, I've got to get out of here. Out of here, I tell you! I can't really explain, it's just that I'm:

a) Acrophobic-   Fearful of heights
b) Aerophobic-   Nervous about breathing used air
c) Agoraphobic-   Frightened by soft sweaters
d) Bibliophobic-   Scared of books, boy you have a lot!
e) Brontophobic-   Chronically afraid of the Flintstones
f) Claustrophobic-   Worried a Von Bulow will kill me
g) Ergophobic-   Frightened of jumping to conclusions
h) Japophobic-   Worried about overdressing
i) I, Phobic-   Fearful of PBS Specials
j) Lyssophobic-   Scared by household cleaning supplies
k) Phobophobic-   Fearful of having a fear
l) Pyropobic-   Frightened by oven tempered cookware
m) Teleophobic-   Fearful of running into Telly Savalas
n) Zenophobic-   Scared to death of American television sets

＊

Gee, I think I'd better leave. All of a sudden I have:
a) A terrible headache

38

b) A miserable toothache
c) Incredible gas
d) Leprosy

You know, I'm really having trouble remembering if I put out my cigarette when I left my house. Am I being crazy? I'm sure I did. No I'm not. I'd better get home and make sure the house isn't up in flames.

I've really got to get going, I'm supposed to get up at 4 A.M. tomorrow to go:
a) Whale harpooning
b) Buffalo Hunting

c) Stand on line for "The Price Is Right"

Did I tell you the doctor put me on a special diet? Well, I have this rare disease and can only eat very specific foods. Oh, it's time for a meal. Do you have any carrot puree with ginseng? You don't? You're kidding. Listen, I'd better get to a health food store or there's no telling what'll happen to me.

My God, it's a full moon! Look, there are a couple of things about myself I never told you, but I don't think right now is the time to get into it, so I'd better be going. Incidentally, do you have any dog bones I could munch on for the ride home?

Holy Mackerel!!! I've got to go, I just realized I forgot to:
a) Turn off the iron
b) Turn on the burglar alarm
c) Plug in my grandmother's kidney dialysis machine

Oh, no . . . I think I'm having a recurrence of some LSD that I took a few years ago. My God, you're wall paper is moving. Don't you see that? I'd better be going. No, you don't have to show me to the door. You just stay where you are and entertain that small man coming out of your nose.

THE OTHER HALF OF TODAY'S
MOST POPULAR FIBS

THE POPULAR LIE

THE OTHER HALF

No salesman will call . . . . He'll just come directly to your home everyday for the next six years.

The doctor will be right with you . . . . After he checks out of that raunchy motel with his wife's best friend, calls his broker, and catches the 4:30 re-run of "Dance Fever."

This won't hurt a bit . . . . If you happen to be Conan The Destroyer.

I'm sorry, he's in a meeting right now, but if you leave your name and number he'll call you right back . . . . After he retires.

This meal was absolutely delicious, I must have the recipe	So I can sell it to Soviet spies for chemical warfare.
My God, you lost weight ...	Now you only look like **half** a side of beef.
You look fabulous	For a pig.

GUT WRENCHING EXPLANATIONS
FOR WHY THE CHECK BOUNCED

I'm just infuriated, and I'm sorry you have to be inconvenienced, but when I returned the clock-radio the bank gave me as a gift, they interpreted it incorrectly and closed my account. Really, the clock didn't keep time so well, but I certainly had no intention of changing banks. Besides, the hot roller set works like a dream.

It was a crying shame. I had written a check to a local merchant and you know what he did? He changed the decimal point and altered the check from fifty to five thousand dollars. He's in jail now, thank God, and as soon as I pick up the money I'll be able to write you a new check. By the way, could you give me a lift to Attica?

The bank inadvertently credited my deposit to someone they claim had a very similar name. Well, I looked into it and found out that a man named Vladimir Boroshov got all my money. I don't think that name sounds like mine, do you?

I know this is going to sound crazy, but some clerk at the bank took an immediate dislike to me after I accidentally hit him in the head with a large loaf of Italian Bread. Now, obsessed with revenge, he purposely bounced all my checks. The bank manager is aware of it and, though he waives the service charges, he can't really fire the guy. You know those unions!

Karl Marx appeared to my spouse in a dream and filled his (her) head with guilt about our Bourgeois lifestyle. Well, the next thing I knew, he (she) emptied our joint checking account, put the money in sacks of five and tens, then walked through the streets distributing the money to bag ladies and bums. Take it from me, be glad you're single.

I find myself in a most interesting dilemma. Actually, my secretary, and I can't understand this because she's been with me for years, took it upon herself to cash my paycheck and run off to the Poconos with my money. I thought she was out ill this week, but police tell me they lost her somewhere near the Mount Airy Lodge.

If only you knew what I've been through. A teller at the bank transferred all my money into Lire. Can you imagine? Then, to make matters worse, he wired it to some little old man who owns a failing bakery in Rome. The man thought it was a godsend and offered me a lifetime supply of Italian baked goods. Obviously, I can't cover the check, but how about a few dozen Canolis? They really are quite good.

I realize this may have been a bit irresponsible, but I mailed you the check before I had a chance to make a deposit. Then, on my way over to the bank, I was kidnapped and buried alive for over a week. It was absolutely terrifying, but you know, I discovered one startling fact—mud makes a lovely dessert topping!

Two weeks ago a man broke into my mother's house and attacked her right in her own living room. She . . . well, she grabbed the nearest object to defend herself . . . and she killed him with the iron. That's right. She actually ironed a man to death. The point is I had to use every last cent for bail and it just cleaned out my checking account. What would you have done if it was your mother? I'm just glad she was too proud to use a dry cleaner.

I'm really quite sorry, but my wife decided to pay off the entire mortgage on the house and neglected to tell me. Naturally, this all but wiped us out, and now I owe overdraft checking $132,000. Listen, you need a maid? My wife does things with an electric broom that you just wouldn't believe.

You think you've got problems? My paycheck bounced!

EXCUSES IN THE PROFESSIONAL WORLD

Have you ever noticed that some people are shiftier than others? Sure, there are the obvious well-educated con artists like lawyers, real estate brokers, and shop-at-home upholstery salesmen. But what about all the other people you come in contact with day after day? How honest are they? Who can you trust? The following table will help you decide:

OCCUPATION	AVG # EXCUSES TOLD PER DAY	USUALLY RELATING TO THE FOLLOWING
Dry Cleaners	162	Why the plastic looks better pressed than your suit.
Maitre 'ds	188	Why that exotic, new herb in your salad looks exactly like a pubic hair.
Travel Agents	523	The fact that they've sent hundreds of people to that resort and no one mentioned a thing about flying rats.
Plastic Surgeons	227	Why he purposely left your nostrils looking like the entrance to the Holland Tunnel.
Tax Accountants	313	Why you won't find jail all that bad.

Hairdressers 192 How fabulous you'll look after he styles your hair with a blow-torch.

ALL IN A DAY'S WORK
A GUIDE TO JOB TITLES
AND WHAT THEY REALLY MEAN

JOB TITLE	WHAT IT REALLY MEANS
Domestic Engineer	Housewife
Cosmetologist	Hairdresser
Lawyer	Carpetbagger
Administrative Assistant	Secretary
Interior Designer	Homosexual
Croupier	Card Dealer
Chiropracter	Voo Doo doctor
Professional Escort	Hooker
FBI Agent	CIA Agent
CIA Agent	Spy
Spy	Overrated Policeman
Policewoman	Lesbian
Dentist	Sadist
Plumber	Extortionist
Auto mechanic	Ex-Con
Actor	Waiter
Singer	Waiter
Dancer	Waiter
Waiter	An Old Actor, Singer, or Dancer

SIMPLE REASONS FOR NOT HAVING
THAT PAPER OR REPORT

I saw this incredibly large waterbug crawling up the leg of the kitchen table this morning. You know what? It's now on page six of that report. (Pick up a large cluster of papers.) You still want it?

I had an office temp come in so the report would be completed on time. Well, wait till you hear this, those idiots sent me a woman from Costa Rica and she typed the entire thing in Spanish. Do you believe it? I was just on my way to get another typist. Adios!

Was I supposed to do that report?

My God!!! The report! (Start hunting through your briefcase.) Oh no! I was reading it over when the 8:15 pulled in a little early. Jeez! I must've thrown it out instead of my cinnamon Danish. (Pull out a half-eaten pastry.)

A paper shredder salesman came to my office to demonstrate one of their new speedy shredders. I told him I really wasn't interested but he refused to listen. Instead, he sets the entire thing up, and before I could say a word, takes the report and makes mincemeat out of it. I was absolutely furious and nearly beat him to a pulp. That guy's damn lucky he gave me such a good deal on an encyclopedia or, I swear, he'd be dead right now.

I was recording the report on my Dictaphone when I was interrupted by a phone call from my doctor. I was so worried about the test results that I forgot to turn the machine off. The next thing I knew my secretary typed it right into the report. To tell you the truth, I just don't think that my prostate irregularities belong in the middle of a report on the advantages of divesting oil resources in the middle-east. (Excuse yourself to go to the bathroom.)

I just had the most frustrating experience. I went out and rented a brand new typewriter so the report would be just perfect. After typing for about two hours, I looked up and noticed the entire thing was filled with these crazy dots. I guess I accidentally rented a Braille typewriter. Don't worry, though, that blind man who sells pencils on the sidewalk said he'd translate at the meeting.

I don't know what came over me, but I accidentally mailed the report with my phone bill. I just called the phone company and some woman named Laverna told me she'd look for it right after she gets back from vacation. There's really no choice, she's the only one who can look for it. It's some kind of union thing. I knew breaking up the phone company was a big mistake!

The wildest thing happened this morning. I was at the train station and when I went to buy a paper I put my briefcase down. Anyway, without my knowing it, someone made a "switch" and took **my** briefcase. I thought I was smack in the middle of some spy ring . . . until I pried it open and **discovered** it was filled with Xerox supplies. Anyway, the guy's in Schenectady fixing a copier and promised to exchange cases in the morning.

The report? I gave it to you. Yes I did, don't you remember? I handed it to you when you walked in this morning. Well, I don't know why I waste time doing reports if you're just going to lose them. (Requires gall and theatrics.)

It fell in the toilet. Believe me, you wouldn't want it now.

You know, I thought the report would have much greater impact if it was oral. Hey, wanna hear the opening?

EXCUSES AND YOUR STATE OF MIND

It's been proved that certain substances will actually help you in inventing truly clever stories while others will cause you to spill the beans and tell the whole truth and nothing but the truth. It's important to familiarize yourself with these substances so there are no unfortunate accidents.

Things that will generally help you make you good stories	Things that will probably make you tell the truth
Tequilla	Liquid Valium
Vodka	Milk of Magnesia
Marijuana	Sodium Pentathol
L.S.D.*	Midnight Visits from God
Peruvian guava root	Recurring nightmares involving Arthur Godfrey**

*Though inventive, stories concocted under the influence of L.S.D. are usually of no value to you or anyone else. It should be noted, however, that some of these stories have been sold to British Television.

**Usually the result of too much L.S.D.

It's important to recognize that different parts of the country require different treatments of your excuse. Dialects, way of life, and differing time zones all come into play when you're on the road. For example, in certain sections of Brooklyn, large breasts are usually referred to as "Kanakas." But if you're in Hawaii and tell someone you were late because you were knocked over by a fat woman with huge "kanakas," you're now talking about a woman with two large natives by her side, most probably Jack Lord and Don Ho. In certain cities some excuses add up to a star performance while in others you'd get laughed right out of town. We've illustrated some of the reasons you could be late in several major cities.

Los Angeles   Had to attend the funeral of a dog who accidentally boiled to death in a hot tub.

New York	The roaches built a barricade using old roach motels and wouldn't let you out the front door.
Miami	An old Jewish lady got in a fight with a coke dealer and you had to save him from a flying rib roast.
New Jersey	Someone accidentally spilled toxic waste on your suit.
San Francisco	You had an uncontrollable urge to redecorate.
Washington	You had to shake an FBI tail.
Baltimore	You had to shake the FBI tail you picked up in Washington.
Las Vegas	You got neon poisoning.
Dallas	You drove to the other end of a shopping center parking lot and ended up in Houston.
Houston	You stopped to ask directions but nobody lives there anymore.

UNFORTUNATE CIRCUMSTANCES
WHICH CAUSED YOU TO GAIN WEIGHT

It seems that I've been having a bizarre psychological reaction to stress that's resulted in sleep-eating. They call it Consomnia. No, I've never heard of it before either, but the doctors tell me that I wake up in the middle of the night, eat a healthy portion of anything that isn't moving, then go back to sleep. Take it from me, it's pure hell!

You'll never believe this but I swallowed some tomato seeds and, for some crazy reason, they've taken root in my stomach. The doctors say the young sprouts are bound to die. I mean, it can't be very sunny down there.

It's true, I gained a few pounds since you last saw me, but you don't know what else happened—I was kidnapped. That's right, kidnapped by a group of out-patients from a nearby mental hospital. They held me captive in a reconditioned bus and force fed me Godiva chocolates for nearly a month.

There was this new place by the office that advertised low calorie cheeseburgers, only 200 calories each—including the french fries! Can you imagine? They were simply delicious and I ate them everyday for lunch. Sometimes for dinner too! The next thing I knew the guy's in jail for fraud and I'm the size of a house. I should've known it was too good to be true. I was eating 1500 calorie lunches . . . plus dessert! Who knew?

About two months ago I had a terrible fall, and it seems my thyroid gland slipped from my neck to my elbow. I don't have to tell you that nothing seems to get burned up anymore . . . except my tailor, he's got to keep letting everything out.

I accidentally swallowed my mother-in-law's fur coat.

I guess I've just been eating more because:
a) I am depressed
b) I'm about to be depressed
c) I'm not depressed anymore
d) My mother is depressed
e) The economy is depressed

I heard some jerk on a morning talk show say that peanut butter isn't fattening. Who knows, maybe I wanted to believe him, but I ate it like wild until I noticed that my queen size bed didn't seem to fit anymore.

I replaced my ex-lover with a new lover—eggplant parmesan!

Didn't you hear? The Jane Russell look is coming back. You better start eating, too, honey, or you'll be out, out, out!

I didn't gain weight, I used a new detergent and all my clothes shrunk. I should have listened to my mother; only do a cold wash.

I've decided to leave my job at the bank and become a Sumo wrestler. What do you think . . . How do I look?

I discovered there's a lot of money in certain areas of modeling. Thank God my brother-in-law's got connections. Today, I'm one of the highest paid "before" models in the business.

Why did I gain weight? That's a stupid question. I'm eating more.

ADVICE FROM THE EXPERTS

Always have several trustcd flunkies to provide you with ironclad alibis.

Become known for your large and deranged family.

Do not lie in a court of law. Unless of course you work there and happen to be late.

If your hands shake when you lie, put them in your pockets. If you don't have pockets, tie them with bakery string and explain it as the latest craze in Paris.

Watch soap operas to get a feel for relentless tragedy.

Be certain not to repeat the same excuse to the same person. That would be stupid.

Become known for your poor medical history.

Never make up an excuse based on an anonymous woman—call her Shirley.

If you happen to flub in the middle, do not panic. Just fall to the floor and pretend you've had a heart attack.

Do not lie on religious holidays—why tempt fate?

Play poker to develop a straight face.

You may be interrogated. Develop a complete and detailed fact pattern.

Fabricate a spouse (roommate, kids) by purchasing a frame and not removing the picture.

Avoid wearing black. Brighter colors are less sinister.

Polyester may cause suspicious sweat. Always wear natural fibers.

If your excuse is challenged; deny, deny, deny! If still challenged, throw up immediately and divert all attention to your health.

Develop the kind of personality people consider psychopathic, but lovable.

Never lie with an eggplant on your head.

Remember Abscam—exercise discretion.

Distract the listener. Have a small, unidentifiable object hanging from your nose.

Learn how to burst into tears.

Never lie to a dead person. It's a waste of time. Besides, if they can hear you, they probably know the truth anyway.

Jot down your story in a little book. You may be questioned days later.

Become known as a cursed person.

The Surgeon General has determined that more than five excuses a day **is** hazardous to your health.

THE WHITE LIE VS. THE BLACK LIE

WHITE LIE
I'm so sorry I'm late, but the car had a flat and it took hours for the auto club to arrive and fix it.

BLACK LIE*
She-e-e-t, I'z late. Buts that cah that I'z stow done wents and got a flat ti-ah. It done took me all but a day to goes steal mah-self anotha honkey cah!

*The authors intend no offense in the writing of the black lie, but will just do anything for a joke. To show you their good intentions they offer the following:

Polish Lie- I'm sorry I'm late but I locked the keys in the car, and the really scary part was that my wife & kids were trapped inside.

Jewish Lie- Late, I'm not late, your early.

Italian Lie- Sorry I'm late but there's a contract out on my life and I had to take the long route.

WASP Lie- WASPS aren't late.

PRESCRIPTION VACATIONS

Whether it's a day at the beach or that dream cruise to Maui, a handful of great illnesses make anything possible. Unlike more traditional human tragedies such as ingrown toe nails, these illnesses escape detection by modern medicine. And they reoccur! So use them over and over again, without fear of getting caught.

ILLNESS	NECESSARY EQUIPMENT
Whiplash	Neck brace or a turtleneck stuffed with toilet paper.
Bad Back	A six-position portable hump.
Allergies	Peel and stick hives.

Trick Knee	A cane and a pair of brightly colored orthopedic shoes, preferably of different heights.
Migraine Headaches	Sunglasses and a bad hairdo.

SEEMINGLY PLAUSIBLE REASONS
FOR ENDING YOUR RELATIONSHIP

The thing is, and I've thought it over very carefully, I'm basically a nudist at heart. If you want to continue our relationship, fine! But you'll have to agree to live with me in a nudist colony. And I think you should go there first, for six months, just to prove your intentions are sincere.

Look, it'll never work. It's totally impossible . . . See, I just can't go to the bathroom when anybody else is in the house.

Now that we're getting serious . . . . , I feel I have to tell you something about myself. If it's too much for you to handle, then it's best we end it now, so please be truthful. I love you, but for some strange psychological reason, I also enjoy having sex with:
a) My brother/sister/father/mother
b) Hefty bags
c) Chihuahuas
d) Dead people

I have decided to convert and become a Mormon. Not only will I give up premarital sex, but I plan to only date other Mormons and may be moving to Utah shortly. Did I ever show you that photo of me with Donny and Marie?

I am only telling you this because I feel you are the kind of fine, mature person who can handle it. Well, here goes. I'm having a sex change. That's right. In fact, I've already started taking testosterone (progesterone). Oh, can I borrow that new pink dress (blue suit)? I think it's really me!

For quite a while now, a man (woman) from another planet has been visiting me in my dreams. We have fallen deeply in love and last night he told me that I must relinquish all my earthly ties and prepare for him to come take me away.

I'm sorry, but I just can't love a person who doesn't worship Glen Campbell.

I've just found out that my great Aunt Louise is going to cut me out of her will if I continue to be seriously involved with anyone. What can I say, the woman hasn't been all "there"

since she got her head caught in an escalator, but it's all rumored that she's leaving me a $100,000 villa in France. Maybe we can get together after she dies?

It's very difficult to explain this to people, but I am severely allergic to sperm. If you can handle total abstinence, so can I. What do you think?

I just discovered that my real mother is the Queen of England. Isn't that unbelievable? Anyway, I'm off to London to live with Mom. Naturally, I'd love to take you with me but, well, you know how royalty can be about these things. My God, I hope the tiara doesn't ruin my hair.

You know, I never really noticed how ugly you are.

This is going to sound bizarre, but my ex-husband (wife, fiance, etc.), who I thought was dead, has suddenly turned up in Iowa and is coming home. Obviously, we'll have to stop seeing each other. I wonder, though, do I have to return all that money to the insurance company?

Would you mind terribly if when we had sex, I wrapped a snake around your neck?

I was waiting for the bus the other day and I stepped into the army recruiting office to get out of the rain. I was chatting with the guy for a while until somehow, and I'm not quite sure how, I enlisted. See you in about four years.

ABSOLUTELY LEGAL REASONS FOR
EXCEEDING THE SPEED LIMIT

Oh officer, my God, I was being tailed by a group of men—ugly, horrible looking men with guns. They were purposely smashing into my car, trying to knock me off the road. I figured the only way I could save my life was to go as fast as possible and hope that a policeman would rescue me. Thank you so much officer, as soon as they saw you they got off the road. By the way, did you happen to notice the car that just got off at the last exit? I'd like to press charges.

Pretend you're deaf and can't hear a word the officer is saying . . .

I'm so stupid! I thought the sign saying 55 meant how many more minutes the highway was open. I was rushing to get to my hotel before they closed down the roads. I'm from out of town, you know. Very out of town.

Officer! My wife fell out of the car and rolled down the hill about a half-mile back. I'm going to see if she's still alive. You get the ambulance . . . I'll meet you there.

Boy, am I glad to see **you**, officer! I could have sworn I just saw a child, bound and gagged, in the car that just passed me. I was speeding up to tail them myself, but now that you're here, I'll let you take over.

YOU'RE NOT GOING TO BELIEVE THIS . . . I JUST SAW THE FLYING NUN SOAR BY!!! Yes, it's unbelievable, but she just flew by. Well, my wife just loves her and I thought I'd try to catch up and get her autograph.

Officer, this is all very simple to explain. You see, I noticed that my car was on fire and rather than stop, I decided to speed up and let the increase in wind velocity put it out (Get out of car, stand back and look carefully.) It worked, By God, it worked! I simply must be going. I must tell my colleagues of this remarkable scientific discovery.

(Panicked) Officer, I just realized I left home without my American Express card. I was rushing home to get it.

I just heard on the news that my parents are being held hostage in a Chinese Laundry by some hanger salesman who

71

completely snapped. He's threatening to kill them both and I've got to get down there. Didn't you hear about it on the news. No? Well I think you should spend a little more time listening to the radio and less time stopping would-be orphans for no reasons at all (drive off in a huff).

Thanks a lot, officer, I was trying for the world record of speeding on a highway without getting stopped. Five more minutes and I would've made it in the Guiness World Book of Records. Now I have to start the whole damn thing over again. You know, I hope you don't think I'm being too forward, but don't you think an apology is in order?

BRILLIANT EXPLANATIONS FOR KILLING
THE DOG OR CAT

You know, the dog/cat really looked like a pillow when I hurled my body onto the couch!

I don't know why, but I thought a Clorox bath would've cleaned her up real nice . . . Who would've guessed? They really ought to put labels on these things.

I didn't know dogs/cats were flammable!

Unmarried, no job, no education . . . It was a clear cut case of euthanasia. I just thought he'd be better off.

Look, anyone can drop a thirty pound turkey. It's not my fault (fill in name of pet) was standing right at my feet.

Gee, I noticed little (fill in name of pet) was looking a little skinny. I thought **you** were feeding her!

Fool! That was no dog/cat! That was THE DEVIL INCARNATE! Yes, I know, but you have to face facts . . . that animal was possessed!

If I had only seen (fill in name of pet) playing in the pot when I replanted the ficas tree, perhaps this tragedy could have been avoided.

Now look me in the eye and tell me that you think I would purposely turn on the oven knowing that little (fill in name of pet) was sleeping in the broiler!

Listen, in that position he looked like a part of the rug. Besides, who would ever think that a vacuum cleaner could do such damage?

I'm sorry, you're right. I should have been more attentive when I saw the steamroller coming. Look at it this way, now we have a lovely bathmat.

Go ahead, blame me. Blame me because Drano happens to look like a can of dog food. Honestly, you'd think I did it on purpose.

I know . . . I know . . . I should have realized that (fill in name of pet) likes to drink water out of the toilet. He's so small, though, and I really didn't see him when I flushed the damn thing. You think we oughta get a plumber?

O.K., I should have been a little more attentive when I was mowing the lawn. But (fill in name of pet) is so furry, I never once thought he wasn't just another weed. I swear!

I figured out why they don't let pets into the supermarket . . . before I knew what was happening, (fill in name of pet) had jumped into the deli slicer and, well, want a cold cut?

HOW TO TALK YOURSELF OUT FROM BETWEEN A ROCK AND A HARD PLACE

A good excuse-maker is always prepared in case someone questions the validity of his story. Even the world's greatest excuse-makers raise an eyebrow or two with a complicated tale. The trick is knowing how to shift the focus of the conversation onto something else.
For example:

WHEN A PERSON

YOU SHOULD

Seems perplexed and doubts your story

Begin to ramble hundreds of irrelevant facts to confuse the listener.

Uncovers one small fact in your story which would make the entire thing untrue

Start to cry and mumble how you were unloved as a child.

Uncovers several small facts in your story which would make the entire thing untrue

Demand to know if you're being called a liar and question the integrity of a relationship where anything you say is scrutinized and believed to be untrue.

| Has iron-clad proof that everything you just said was a complete lie | Immediately accuse that person of doing something far worse than lying and shift the focus of the conversation to the accuser's cruel and selfish streak. |

EXCELLENT REASONS FOR GETTING OFF THE PHONE

I really can't talk right now, I'm right in the middle of:
a) a good sleep
b) a good book
c) a good T.V. show
d) two steamy men

Oh hi, (cough) listen I have (cough) a potato chip (cough) wedged in my throat (cough) and I really can't (cough) talk, let me (cough) call you back later (cough).

OH MY GOD!!! The drapes are on fire! . . . What? . . . Hold on . . . No . . . Help! Bye.

GROSS! (sputter, cough, and generally rearrange your phlegm) You won't believe what I just did! UGH! I just took a sip out of a can of Coke with a cigarette butt in it. Oh jeez, I'm getting sick . . . Let me call you later.

I really can't talk right now, I've finally managed to sit down and:
a) pay all the bills
b) balance my checkbook
c) re-copy my phone book
d) answer a personal ad
e) place a personal ad
f) iron a wedding gown

Oh hi, look, don't ask, but I've got a bat caught in my hair. It's really vile and oh, God, I think I'm going to pass out. I've gotta go.

(In very excited tone) Hi, Hi, this is too much. I can't believe you just called. I'm so excited (shriek with delight) Ed McMahon just announced my name on the Tonight Show as the winner of the American Family Publisher's Sweepstakes!! I could just die! Oh, wait! Should I take the dream house or the cash? I don't know what to do . . . Let me call my accountant and I'll get back to you. Bye!

(In a whisper) Hi . . . Shh! I just found out that the FBI is tapping my phone. They think I'm involved in a multi-million dollar coupon fraud ring. Honestly, I never thought sneaking a coupon for family size Fab would get me in this much trouble. Damn, I knew that cashier in a trench coat looked suspicious. Anyway, let's talk later.

Hello? Hello? Is anybody there? Hell? Look, if you don't stop calling, I'm going to contact the police. Hello? Goodbye! (slam down the phone and leave off the hook).

Oh, hi. Can I call you back, I was just on my way to:
a) a cocktail party
b) a dinner party
c) a tupperware party

Alo? Alo? ooh you weesh to spik to? ooh? Yo hablo espanola? No? ooh? Oh! Dees not hee. Nono hee. Adios.

Oops, there's the doorbell! I'll call you later.

MEETING YOUR MATCH:
HOW TO TELL IF SOMEONE IS HANDING
YOU A LINE

There's more to effective excuse-making than making up a great excuse on the spot. A clever, quick-minded opponent can easily "out-excuse you." It's important a develop a knack for spotting anyone who might be trying to pull a fast one. Once you do, you'll be able to pull an even faster one. And who knows, with enough practice, you might even get a high paying job as head of luggage claims for a major airline.

HE CANNOT LOOK YOU IN THE EYE: One of the best ways to spot an excuse in action. You can be sure that a person who cannot look you in the eye is a person who is not telling the truth. Eyes are classic "whistle-blowers" and will tell you if someone is fibbing faster than bamboo-under-the-fingernail kits, body stretch racks, and all the other fine products made by the Medieval Torture Supply & Equipment Corp. of Nutley, New Jersey. This truism may be based on a little known ancient superstition, a deep-rooted mass psychological fear, that if you look at someone directly in the eye when telling a lie, yours will fall right out of your head.

HE GETS CONFUSED: One of the easiest ways to spot a phony story. If a person's saga seems all out of whack, ask a few pointed questions. If he can't get the facts straight, then you're being conned. Keep in mind, though, confusion is not always due to a lie. For example, if a person doesn't pick you up for work because he claims his car broke down and later cites three unrelated mechanical problems, then chances are he's handing you a line. But, if a person doesn't pick you up because he claims his late Aunt Rose borrowed the car, this is not called an excuse. It's called senility.

HE SWEATS PROFUSELY: If you happen to notice that a person looks like he just stepped out of a Jacuzzi, and it's not August in Dallas, then chances are he's telling you a good story. Sweating is a psychological reaction to stress, lying, or a very cheap deodorant. Ancient scriptures reveal that humans perspire in these situations due to a genetic fail-safe based on the assumption that when a person starts to sweat buckets, people will be too grossed out to care if he's lying.

HE BITES HIS NAILS: Another "stress-related" signal, a nail biter is, more often than not, telling you an excuse. Either that or they're on a very strict diet.

HE BITES YOUR NAILS: This is not only a dead give away that the person is lying, and lying big, but it's also a sign that the person is in desperate need of a few weeks rest at the Sunnyvale Home.

HIS EYES TURN RED, LIGHTENING FLASHES, AND HE LAUGHS A LOT LIKE THE DEVIL: This is a strong indication that the person is not exactly known for telling the truth . . . ever! In this situation, it is recommended that you leave immediately and seek asylum in the nearest religious retreat.

EASY-TO-USE EXPLANATIONS FOR NOT RETURNING A CALL

You know, I tried to call you back, but every single time I dialed your number I kept getting some Chinese man who said my Lo Mein was on the way.

I don't know what came over me, but I sat down on the couch to watch HBO and the next thing I knew it was 4:30 in the morning. You know what? The same movie was still on! Is that unbelievable? They never change those damn movies!

Oh, I was going to call you back but the most terrifying thing happened—I came down with a temporary case of lockjaw. I mean, that wasn't even really the bad part. Every time I tried to talk I drooled on myself. You should see that new shirt I bought, UGH!

To tell you the truth, the dial fell off my phone.

The operator called and told me to leave my line clear for a call from the mid-east. I just couldn't imagine who'd be calling me, so I sat there like a jerk for hours. Meanwhile, no one ever called, and to make matters worse, I blew a chance to win a portable hot tub in a radio contest!

My two front caps fell out of my mouth . . . and every time I tried to speak I sounded like Elmer Fudd.

This really gruesome creature made its way into the house and took an unusual liking to my phone. It was bigger than a roach, just as disgusting, but smaller than a rat. Oh, you don't want to know. Anyway, I wasn't going near that thing for anything! Thank God it finally left after unsuccessfully trying to mate with my trimline.

I must've called you back a million times and it was constantly busy. What the hell were you doing? Reading *Kane and Abel* to a friend?

Gee, didn't anyone tell you I was suddenly called for jury duty? Yeah, the deliberation got so heated that we were sequestered at the Airport Motor Inn . . . what a dump! Hey, need some soap?

MAKING THE BEST OF A BAD SITUATION:
A GUIDE TO SOLVING SOME EVERYDAY PROBLEMS

EVERYDAY PROBLEM	HOW BEST HANDLED
Late to office	Excuse

Miss friend's funeral	Excuse

Forget wife's birthday	Excuse

Lover found sleeping with your best friend	Gun

Right as I was about to call you my mother called, convinced there was an intruder in the house. You know my mother. Anyway, she made me stay on the phone for at least an hour while she patrolled the house with a can of hair spray. By the time she let me go, I was so tired, not to mention starving, that I went right to bed.

I called the deli to order a sandwich and some idiot never hung up the phone. I kept screaming into the receiver "Hang Up, Hang UP!" But all night I was forced to listen to the intricacies of the Moscowitz wedding. Corned Beef at a wedding, could you die?

While I was in the shower someone stole all the phones.

HANDY STORIES FOR BREAKING A DATE

This is going to sound really strange, but I've got a Q-Tip stuck in my ear and I'm on the way to the emergency room. Only me, right? What? What did you say?

Gee, I feel awful having to explain this, but I was giving my hair a hot oil treatment. Well, I didn't know you weren't supposed to use Mazola, and now I can't get it out of my hair! I've already tried Comet, and it still won't come out. Anyway, I look like I had some kind of bizarre brain surgery or something and I'm not going anywhere!

I've never told you this but I'm a freelance envelope stuffer. As with any pressure-important field, I'm on call 24 hours a day, seven days a week. Anyway, a really important job just came in for a mail-order bible operation out of Tennessee and I've got to get right to work.

Look, I have to pinch hit for a friend who sells vacation land in the Poconos. She's sick and they told her if she didn't find a replacement she'd lose her job. Hey, interested in buying an acre or two? I get 10%!

Guess what? My foster child has just arrived to visit me. Isn't that sensational? He came all the way from Zonglodunk so I'll have to cancel our plans. Gee, you think Bloomingdales might be too much of a culture shock for him?

This is wild, but I just got a call from my father and it seems my grandfather has escaped from his nursing home. We're arranging a family posse and I've got to cover midtown, looking for an old man in striped pajamas. I wonder, where would you be if you were senile and on the loose?

This is a little embarrassing, but I'll have to break our date. You see, well, I was in the mood for some chocolate, and I kinda ate an entire bar. Thing is, when I looked at the wrapper to check the name, it was **that** good, I noticed it wasn't Hershey's . . . It was EX-LAX! Now I'm afraid to leave the house, much less the bathroom. Ohh, gotta go!

I just found out this is the night my family is on "Family Feud." Anyway, my mom is kind of having a little get together and I really have to go. I'd ask you to join us but it might get a little tense. You see, my Uncle Milton blew the bonus game and now my mother blames him for not being able to re-do her living room. I'll call you tomorrow.

There's a man standing outside on my ledge threatening to jump, and I really feel it would be irresponsible of me to leave the house without trying to talk him in. The problem is, after what he's already told me, I think he's better off jumping.

Listen, I'm sorry I have to break our date on such short notice, but our doorman had a heart attack. Now, all the tenants have to rotate as make-shift doorman, and guess what? I got tonight! Listen, to make it up to you I'll take you to dinner on tonight's tips. I heard Saturday is a gold mine!

LIVING, LOVING, LYING:
THE IMPORTANCE OF CREATING AN INTRIGUING,
BUT FALSE, PAST, PRESENT, AND FUTURE

Let's face it. No one wants to marry, or even date, a person with a dull, boring past, insignificant present, or pitiful future. Potential mates seek mystery, romance, adventure, and lots of cash.

So if you're a hairnet weaver in Reading, Pennsylvania, and are stupid enough to reveal this information on dates, then you're almost sure to end up alone on Saturday nights, dreaming of that special cruise on the Love Boat.

"If they want intrigue, give 'em intrigue," said Don Juan, a world famous lover who was, in fact, nothing more than a salad bar supervisor for a chain of all-you-can-eat steak and salad joints in the Southeast.

Historians, in a study commissioned by the Playboy Mansion, have determined that his phenomenal success was largely due to a good cock-and-bull story plus, possibly, a few impressive tricks he learned to do with croutons.

Tell a woman you're an insurance salesman and she won't bat an eye. But tell her you're head of surgery for a major medical institution, and a close personal friend of Frank Sinatra, and she's yours. Not only that, but a wildly inventive

91

past and present opens the door to literally hundreds of excuses day after day.

So go ahead. No one will find out. And if they do, they'll love you too much to care. You hope.

Sorry, I'm late. I got stuck at the office for a last minute paper clip inventory.

You're not going to believe it, I fell asleep on the train/bus and when I woke up it was nearly (fill in time)—but get this . . . I was in the train yard! It took me over an hour just to figure out how to get out of there. It wasn't a total loss, though, I got this terrific poster for Anacin. Wanna frame it?

As a gag, and not a funny one at that, the guys in the office wanted to show me how much I'm overworking. So they tied me to my chair with typewriter ribbon. Then, they went home.

I was out to dinner with my boss at an exclusive restaurant. Well, I . . . I went to the ladies room and on my way back to the table I couldn't help but notice that everyone was laughing hysterically. Then, the Maitr 'd pulled me aside and told me that the back of my dress was tucked into my underwear. I ran out the door immediately and have been wandering the streets aimlessly, crying for hours. I AM TOTALLY HUMILIATED AND WANT TO DIE!

I had to run down to my mother's house to help her move the oven. Next thing I know I'm eating roast chicken, then she chewed my ear off and wouldn't let me leave till Johnny Carson finished his monologue.

I was sitting at a red light in my car, you know, minding my own business, when all of a sudden this guy with a gun gets in and takes control of the wheel. Turns out he just robbed a bank and I was part of an all night police chase. It was just like the French Connection. Then, of course, it took forever to convince the police that I wasn't his accomplice—even though I have to admit we did get pretty chummy.

I got locked in the bathroom at the office.

I was on line in the supermarket and I put my bag/attache case on the conveyor belt, you know, the one with the long strap. Next thing I know, the cashier starts the damn thing. The strap got wedged in between the belt and a can of DelMonte Pizza Sticks. They had to take the entire thing apart. Then, they had the audacity to want to charge me for repairs. Could you imagine? I'm never going to that store again. Well, except for maybe double coupon days.

While I was driving home, all four wheels fell off the car.

I did some last minute shopping and while I was frantically trying on a (fill in anything you're likely to buy) they closed the store. I couldn't believe it. I spent the entire night locked in a dressing room wondering if that story about Doberman Pincers roaming the store is true.

I don't know what came over me, but I went to our old apartment by mistake. I spent the entire night banging on the door and wondering why my keys didn't work. I finally called a locksmith and when he opened the door I realized what I had done. I've got to tell you, though, a bunch of pigs moved in. That's for sure.

I took two aspirin because I had this awful headache. Anyway, I don't remember exactly what happened but they went the wrong way and got lodged up my nose. Do you have any idea what that feels like? Anyway, I went to the emergency room and they actually had to douche my nose for (fill in number of hours late). Oh, no. I think I have to sneeze.

I drove (fill in name of business associate) to the airport and after he (she) boarded the plane I realized I still had some important papers. The ground attendants were nice enough to let me dash on the plane, but not bright enough to tell the flight crew to wait. The next thing I knew I was on my way to Grand Rapids, Michigan.

After everyone left the office, I figured I had the chance to do some Xeroxing without being bothered. That line can be unreal during the day. Everything was going well until my tie (scarf) got caught in the feeder and yanked me right into the machine. I screamed for help but it was (fill in number of hours late) until security found me sleeping on the machine.

I took the bus home and when I put my token in, my ring slipped off my finger and into the fare box. Well, you know the driver doesn't have the key to that thing, so I had to go all the way back to the garage so the cashier could open it up. Do you know that bus goes all the way to (fill in destination far away from home) and man it was hard to get home from there.

CREATIVE EXCUSE-MAKING:
DO'S AND DON'TS

Believe it or not, everything that pops into your mind should not be used as the basis of a story. Many different creative situations, though tempting, may raise a suspicious brow. We offer the following list to help you separate the good from the bad.

NO EXCUSE SHOULD INVOLVE	ANY EXCUSE COULD INVOLVE
Alien Spacecraft	Mechanical defects in a Ford
*	
Marauding band of wild lesbians	Eighteen Jewish ladies on their way to a matinee
*	
Dinosaurs	Rabid Schnauzers
*	
Visits from God	Rex Humbard
*	
Lebanese terrorists	Post office employees

98

| Helga the Dominatrix | A dental hygienist |

| Eighteenth Century slave ships | Peoples Express |

SOLID REASONS WHY YOU ARE UMEMPLOYED

Let me put it this way: Nepotism was never a problem for me, until my grandfather got kicked off the board of directors.

My employer confessed his (her) uncontrolled sexual lust for me. I was very flattered, of course, but it did pose a significant problem, considering we're both the same sex.

My company merged with some huge conglomerate and word was that if you wanted to remain on staff, you'd better be willing to relocate to Scranton. I mean, really. I'd rather starve.

I didn't know that WATTS line wasn't for personal use. Thing is I got away with it for years. Until my sister moved to Hawaii, and well, I guess it kind of stuck out.

To be quite honest, and I say this without conceit, I developed a stream-lined organizational structure that eliminated over 300 positions. Problem was, one of them was my boss's. So he fired me.

I noticed that my medical benefits covered psychiatry. So I started to see a shrink, you know, just to see what it's all about. Well, the next thing I knew, my boss told me there was no room in the company for unstable employees. Talk about a catch 22.

So I got a little out of hand at the annual sales meeting and danced naked on the Viennese table. It's the goddamn eighties. Who'd have thought they would fire me.

For a solid year I thought the office opened at ten. Somebody really should have said something a bit sooner. But, without the benefit of the doubt, they just let me go.

Out of work? Not me, I'm self-unemployed.

WHY I CAN'T VISIT YOU, MOM

Absolutely no excuse.

MORE ADVICE FROM THE EXPERTS:

You should now be prepared to tackle virtually any problem that requires a quick-thinking, nifty excuse. But we leave you with more than the ability to get out of absolutely anything. We leave you with another 25 important tips from the experts. If you can't remember anything else from this book, at least remember these few tips. Now that's not too much to ask, is it?

Avoid stuttering, slurring, spitting, and drooling.

For that authoritative edge, always lie standing up.

Learn how to maintain eye contact.

Never lie to a person with a wandering eye. It can be disconcerting.

Develop a close relationship with a doctor in case a medical note is necessary.

Sit on a sea urchin to understand pain.

Avoid sugar. Hyperactivity may cloud the mind.

Study the greats: Richard Nixon, J.R. Ewing, Lucy Ricardo.

Keep all nervous ticks under complete control.

Smoke heavily to develop a nagging, hacking cough.

On sleepless nights count excuses instead of sheep.

Never scratch your head and say ''um.''

For credibility, leave your glasses on. If you don't have any, buy a pair.

For added confidence, carry a gun.

Flaring nostrils have been known to ruin a good excuse.

Do not lie to anyone with a hairlip. It's in very poor taste.

Subscribe to the *National Enquirer*.

Never tell an excuse with a piece of food wedged in between your front teeth.

Eat large quantities of bran to discover the meaning of immediacy.

Avoid lying to a person believed to be mentally unstable and accused of several unprovoked murders with a bowling ball.

Discuss your senile mother at least once a week.

Watch game shows to understand irrational behavior.

Should you begin to lie to yourself, seek professional psychiatric assistance.

For instant pity, set your hair on fire.

Never let anyone know you have this book.

MORE GOOD REASONS WHY YOU WERE LATE

During the night my apartment building shifted, and all the blood ran to my feet. They're O.K. now, but I couldn't get my shoes on for hours.

Last night at Roy Roger's, I was served a Trigger-burger on Dale Evan's buns, I only got over the experience a few hours ago.

Someone took my car for a joy-ride last night. I came out this morning and it was covered with whipped cream, had a cherry on top too. Kids are getting weirder and weirder.

I thought it was daylight savings time and I set my clock back.

I was stuck for three hours with my finger jammed in the coin return of a phone. You'd think they could move a little faster, huh?

My little cousin was spending the night at our house, when she woke up believing she'd been possessed. It took a long time to calm her down and we're still trying to get that gook out of the sheets.

My roommate was drinking Jolt cola and Jack Daniel's last night. I'll be late because if someone doesn't care for him/

her, she might slip into a coma. She called it a Jumpin' Jack Flash.

Last night, my eye popped out while I was coughing. My doctor fixed the problem, but now I want to run out and buy Sammy Davis, Jr. albums.

Damndest thing happened. I was getting ready to leave, when I looked at the cat and all his fur started to fall off. It's not time for him to shed so I took him to the vet.

All of my caps fell out last night during dinner, that's the last time I go to that orthodontist!

As I was leaving my pants got caught in the doorway and ripped right off of me. I wouldn't mind so much if that guy hadn't been so quick with his camera.

My mom claims there is an alien living in her garage, and that he arrived in a strange contraption with lots of lights. Well I checked it out, and it was only Geraldo Rivera in his low-rider.

My pet parakeet suddenly exploded for no reason, pretty bizarre, huh? I guess it's to keep population down.

The couple that moved in next door are from Iran. I've been watching them the past few days. They think we're fooled, they pretend to be moving in furniture and rugs; but I know they're planning an armed uprising.

Remember how I was going to see an acupuncurist about my nagging back? Well it seems he was a novice, and to cut a long story short, I'm sitting here looking like a damn hedgehog.

I went to see a shrink about my incessant depressive moods, and he told me that I had to take a week's holiday in Bermuda. I've been making arrangements, after all, it is for my own good.

I'm going to be late today, I was arrested last night for solicitation. It's all a big misunderstanding, it was the girl **next** to me at the bus stop that was screaming, "Hey, sailor, want a good time."

They finally caught up to me for those unpaid parking tickets. Boy am I gonna get it.

My Uncle George, the one who doubles for Dom DeLouise in his action films, arrived at my house last night absolutely crocked. I threw my back out getting him to the couch.

The cabbie was a PLO terrorist who wanted to kidnap me to his homeland, as a bargaining chip. He let me go when I reminded him that the cab wouldn't get us there.

While I was in the shower, the cat pissed on the only clean towel in the place, so I had to drip-dry before I could leave.

I had a horrible nightmare involving Frank Perdue, some 10,000 Italian waiters, a reactor meltdown, and being trapped in a room with Ollie North. Couldn't sleep a wink.

MORE EXCUSES TO GET THE WHOLE DAY OFF

There was a woman on the train last night who kept staring at me very strangely. When we got off the train she introduced herself as my twin sister, separated at birth. We need time to get to know one another.

My hairpiece fell into the toilet.

A guy got on the subway yesterday and announced he was taking us to Oz. Damned if it didn't work, too. Tough place to catch a ride home from, though.

I have to visit my sick Uncle Herbie. He hasn't been the same since his wife died in that still-unexplained gardening accident.

My father has begun sleepwalking, and I'm always the one who has to keep him from hurting himself. (Or others, last night he had a steak knife and was talking like Norman Bates in *Psycho*.)

Sorry, can't come to work today, I've got running sores over 50% of my upper body. Nothing serious, though.

I dreamt I was a butterfly, but when I woke up, I couldn't be certain if I was a man, who dreamt he was a butterfly; or a butterfly, dreaming he is a man. I was so confused I forgot to go to work.

I accidentally took my wife's No-Doze instead of my vitamins. Butthat'sO.K.I'lljuststayhereanddigtrenchesintheyard, byenow.

My roommate gave me a haircut while I was asleep, I don't think the manager would care for the mohawk.

There's a mouth forming where my belly-button was, and it claims to be the Holy Spirit. Anyway, the boys from the *National Enquirer* are on their way.

My wife just told me that she has been cheating on me for two years, I need time to sort this out. I can't believe it . . . with the bellboy on our honeymoon?!

Every time the circus comes to town, something like this happens: one of their elephants got loose and sat on my car. It was only a VW Bug, it's disappeared.

My second cousin Sylvia, the three-time heiress and current main attraction at Chico's (on 59th), brought over a few of her friends for a party. They should be gone by tomorrow.

My dog buried all of my shoes in the yard, and won't tell me where unless I give him a **whole box** of doggie snacks. I can't get them without the shoes—standoff.

My cat and dog teamed up this morning and made themselves breakfast. But the kitchen is such a mess it'll take all day to clean up. I wonder how they cracked the eggs?

I'm picking up faint traces of cosmic energy, I've got to stay home and try to channel them into my aura. (This is most effective in California.)

I've got a case of 24-hour plague, I'll be in tomorrow.

MORE RANDOM EXCUSES

As before, simply choose one from the "A" column, and one from the "B" to provide yourself with an instant excuse.

A	B
Large hairy man with no neck	Causes you to run off of the road
Woman with a pink doberman	Wakens Godzilla off the coast of New York.
Twelve car pile-up	Take over the office you work
47 Russian Cossacks	Causes hysteria
Sniper with a water-gun	Reminds you of what you shouldn't have done in the sixties
Small blue man in a melty hat and jeweled glasses	Mugs you for the secret microfilm by mistake
Wallpaper salesman from Sascatchuwan	Threatens to have his boys piss on your lawn if you don't pay protection money
Great dane in a limosine	Destroys your car just before you reach it
Mime juggling live grenades	Falls out of the back of a Brink's truck
$100,000 in cash	
Man doing an impersonation of Ronnie and Ollie in the White House steam room	

MORE OF WHY THE CAR IS DENTED

I was in the store buying cigarettes when I heard the sound. Some idiot had gotten out of his car without putting it in park! Got away before I could catch him.

I was driving through a neighborhood where some kids were playing with BB guns, Too bad I didn't find out until too late. Who's going to pay for this?

I was driving past the grocery store when this woman came out and started screaming something about the antichrist; she threw a honeydew melon at the car. Those people are getting out of hand.

I was parked outside the building when someone threw their T.V. out the window. (Size of dent can be altered by size and contact point of T.V.)

These attendants at the market are getting militant! I was wheeling my cart to the car when they started chasing me with carts of their own. I hid in the car but they started slamming into the sides.

I hydroplaned last time we had rain, slid right into a cop about to drink hot coffee, and he threw the book at me. All because of a scalded crotch. Touchy huh?

I was sitting at the corner out there, when this guy in a hockey mask started to attack the car with a chain saw. It's getting dangerous out there!

I went through the toll booth too fast and the attendant opened fire on me! Must think he's Harry Callahan, slammed me against the car so hard it got dented.

A really humongous piece of bird guano, hurtling from its airborn source, stuck the car and dented it. It was a really **tremendously** humongous piece of guano.

I was driving along as carefully as you please, when this guy wearing all leather, and driving the last of the V8 Interceptors, starts slamming into me and screaming about a sequel.

I hit a Hare Krishna on the way home, a real fat one too. But who'll miss him, y'know? I stashed him by the side of the road.

FURTHER REASONS FOR
THAT BILL NOT BEING PAID

I've just been pronounced bankrupt, sorry but you'll have to wait your turn. As soon as I collect an incredibly big check from the government, you'll get your money. I'm changing my name to Chrysler.

I caught my hands in a threshing machine the other day, and subsequently, haven't been in any shape to write large checks (or even small ones). Call me in a month.

Have a friend call, and tell them that you've been admitted to the local mental facility for treatment of your compulsive aggression toward pushy creditors.

My bank had a power surge in their computer system that destroyed most of the files, as soon as they recredit the account I'll send the check along.

Oh! We **thought** that something had slipped out of the mail pouch and down the sewer, but when we looked we couldn't see anything. Who do I make this out to again?

I didn't get any bill! I never received anything of the sort. Must've been lost in the mail. (This is especially effective as the postal service is renowned for its ineptitude.)

I've been meaning to call about that. I bought all that stuff while under hypnosis. See, the therapist I went to was a scam, he used people to buy things for him. I'll be returning most of it unopened as he's been caught, Thank god, this is embarrassing.

MORE REASONS
YOU DON'T HAVE THE REPORT/PAPER

My bag with all the papers and books in it was stolen at the train station.

My secretary has been spending a little too much quality time with her kid, she typed that paper up phonetically. When it's redone, I'll let you know.

Evidently my secretary had the Dictaphone in one ear, and a walkman in the other. The report reads like Ozzy Osbourne wrote for twenty minutes on land use in industry and construction.

Awww, damn! I **knew** I forgot something when I left the library yesterday! (point at another's) There's mine, whoever they are stole it!

The typewriter ran out of ribbon as I finished the 4th page. I couldn't get another at that hour, and besides, what are deadlines anyway but the fragile constructs of our fallible, human brains?

I've decided to do the report in metred rhyme, I was rehearsing all night. It only takes 20 minutes and it's a lot more fun than just **reading** the report. Ready, here's the beginning . . .

It was blown out my window along with my stereo, and several good books. Sure gets windy on the 78th floor.

I think my sister may have picked it up accidentally when she grabbed some stuff off my table. She's back in Colorado now, but I'll have her mail it to me.

My uncle, the hippie, put something unidentifiable into my coffee, and the report turned into an exploration into human consciousness. I'll do it over, and that's the last time **he** visits.

It was eaten by a dog-faced boy.

My briefcase fell open on the street, and before I could collect them all, a bag man collected pages 12 through 49 and started adding them to his collection.

I've been completely apathetic these last few weeks, haven't done much of anything except watch Mr. Ed re-runs. I'll do it if I feel like it. (Takes guts, use carefully.)

MORE REASONS WHY
YOU SUDDENLY GAINED WEIGHT

I stopped metabolizing food about a week ago. So far it's just making me fat, but I could starve to death while I get fatter! Hope they find a cure before I explode.

On a bet in college once, I swallowed a . . .
a) goldfish
b) worm
c) baby boa constrictor

. . . and it seems to have survived and thrived, and grown!

Oh, that's just an illusion created by the clothing, I wouldn't be wearing it at all, except the cleaners are late with my other suits.

Two months ago, I toured an atomic reactor with my science class. I think a radiation leak is making my thyroid gland mutate.

It began raining small, greased watermelon. Never, ever look up during that type of storm, take it from me.

The ultimate fate of mankind burdened me so, that solace could only be found in a Sara Lee cheesecake. Whole.

I was at my friend the rabbi's for dinner last week. Well his wife likes to cook, and likes to feed people even more. Six helpings of chicken soup, and "some for later."

I'm practicing for the part of Buddha in a play for school.

I haven't gained weight, you fool, your eyes are playing tricks with you.

My wife never fully regained her figure after our kids were born, and now she's trying to make me fat in revenge. I've never eaten so well, but I question her motive.

The hypnotherapist I went to to stop smoking did the job, but the side effect is that I now eat uncontrollably instead! I'll sue the bastard.

Do not slur, stutter, drool, or spit during a lie.

Stand when you lie, it gives an authoritative edge to whatever you say.

As has been covered before, eye contact is vital to a convincing deception.

Cultivate the friendship of a professional physician, in the event a note from such is required.

To teach yourself how to fake anguished faces, understand pain by swallowing a handful of rose thorns.

Don't drink too much caffeine or use too much sugar, as being hyperactive won't help your story.

Learn from videotapes of the greats: North, Reagan, Meese, Ralph Kramden, and of course, the infamous—Tricky Dick.

Control those nervous ticks.

If you can't sleep, try making up excuses to pass the time.

Avoid using the term "like" in an excuse, and don't say "um" too often.

Glasses add to the believability of the excuse.

To boost your confidence, trying carrying a large caliber automatic pistol wherever you go, works for me.

Don't, do not, under any circumstances, break out laughing during **any** excuse.

Read the *National Enquirer*, the *Post*, and the *Daily Star* every day.

Try not to have halitosis while lying, it can ruin the whole effect.

If props are required for your excuse, prepare them well ahead of time.

To gain an understanding of immediate need, eat a pan of Ex-Lax brownies.

Develop a nagging cough, smoking a pack or two a day will help.

Never lie to a renowned liar, that would be stupid.

Every so often, mention your sick aunt in Poughkeepsie.

Study game shows to develop an appreciation and understanding of foolishness and irrational behavior.

Never, ever, ever, let **anybody** know you've bought this book, they'll never trust you again.

MORE REASONS WHY
THE RELATIONSHIP HAS TO END

I'm sorry, didn't I tell you that I have a terminal case of ear wax, I'll be a goner within the year.

I don't like this western tradition of monogamy. I think men should have as many wives as they can support. So I'm moving to Arabia, however, you're welcome to join my harem as number one wife.

I'm not interested in seeing you after I discovered that hobby of yours, imagine, blindfolded mountain climbing! Well don't look at me for the next trip.

MORE STORIES FOR BREAKING A DATE

The styling mousse I used turned one half of my head green and the other red. We'll have to take a raincheck on that date until Christmas.

My friend is up with a busted leg, and he needs me to sell his encyclopedias for him. If I don't, he'll lose his job. Can I interest you in a complete set of volumes you will treasure, and give to your kids to learn from?

My grandfather wandered off while we were out at the mall today. Now I've got to look for him. I've been to the video-game parlor already, that leaves Frederick's and the bars.

I needed a chocolate fix badly, and the only stuff in the house was from last Halloween. Now I'm so sick that I can't move.

My uncle the lush came by convinced that it was New Year's Eve. I've got to get rid of the party he brought and then get him dried out. I'll call you tomorrow.

There's a guy on the ledge threatening to jump, I've got to try to talk him down. Although if what he's told me is true, I'd help him more by shoving him off.

I've been locked in the office and I left my keys at home.
Now the guard has released the dobermans inside, so even if I
got out of the building I'd still be trapped, sorry.